Ink and Independence:
The Story of Louisa May Alcott

Louisa May Alcott, the beloved American author, was born on November 29, 1832, in Germantown, Pennsylvania. She was the second of four daughters born to Amos Bronson Alcott, an educator and transcendentalist philosopher, and Abigail May Alcott, a social worker and women's rights advocate. Louisa May Alcott's upbringing was deeply influenced by her family's intellectual pursuits and progressive values.

In 1834, when Louisa was just two years old, her family relocated to Concord, Massachusetts. The town became a center of intellectual and literary activity, with prominent figures like Ralph Waldo Emerson, Henry David Thoreau, and Nathaniel Hawthorne residing there. Louisa's father, Amos Bronson Alcott, was deeply involved in the transcendentalist movement and often hosted discussions with these notable thinkers, exposing Louisa to a stimulating intellectual environment from a young age.

Despite her family's connection to the literary world, the Alcotts faced financial struggles throughout Louisa's childhood. Bronson Alcott's unconventional teaching methods and philosophical pursuits often left the family in precarious financial situations. These early experiences of poverty and the constant need to support her family would greatly shape Louisa's future writing endeavors.

Louisa May Alcott's passion for writing emerged early in her life. As a child, she would create plays and stories for her sisters, Anna, Elizabeth (Beth), and Abigail (May), to perform. Louisa's natural storytelling talent was evident from a young age, and she began submitting her work to various publications when she was just a teenager.

In 1852, Louisa experienced her first taste of literary success when one of her stories was published in the well-known magazine, "Olive Branch." Encouraged by this early recognition, she continued to write and publish short stories and poems in various publications, using pseudonyms such as Flora Fairfield and A.M. Barnard.

Despite her growing success as a writer, Louisa May Alcott faced numerous challenges. Her family's financial struggles persisted, and she often took on various jobs to support them. Alcott worked as a governess, teacher, and seamstress, and she even served as a nurse during the American Civil War. These diverse experiences not only provided Alcott with material for her writing but also shaped her compassionate worldview and strong sense of social justice.

It was during her time as a nurse that Alcott contracted typhoid fever and was forced to return home to Concord. This setback, while detrimental to her physical health, became a turning point in her literary career. Encouraged by her publisher, she began writing a series of letters based on her nursing experiences, which were eventually compiled into the book "Hospital Sketches." Published in 1863, the book garnered critical acclaim and established Alcott as a promising author.

"Little Women" and Literary Legacy

Louisa May Alcott's literary career reached its pinnacle with the publication of her most famous and enduring work, "Little Women." The novel, published in two volumes in 1868 and 1869, captured the hearts of readers around the world and solidified Alcott's place in literary history.

"Little Women" tells the story of the four March sisters — Meg, Jo, Beth, and Amy — and their coming-of-age journeys during the American Civil War era. Drawing inspiration from her own life and family, Alcott infused the characters with depth, relatability, and a spirit of independence that resonated with readers. The novel explored themes of love, friendship, sibling bonds, societal expectations, and the pursuit of personal dreams.

The success of "Little Women" was unprecedented. Readers were captivated by the March sisters and their relatable struggles, and the novel became an instant bestseller. Alcott's depiction of strong, independent female characters challenged traditional gender roles and inspired generations of women to pursue their ambitions and dreams.

Beyond its commercial success, "Little Women" had a profound impact on American literature and culture. Alcott's vivid storytelling, combined with her portrayal of domestic life and the challenges faced by women, elevated the novel to a level of literary importance. It became a significant contribution to the genre of domestic realism, a style of writing that focused on everyday life and the experiences of ordinary people.

The popularity of "Little Women" led to Alcott's continued exploration of the March family in two sequels: "Little Men" (1871) and "Jo's Boys" (1886). These books further developed the characters and expanded on their lives as they grew into adulthood. Although not as widely read as "Little Women," these sequels contributed to Alcott's literary legacy.

Louisa May Alcott's writing career extended beyond the March family saga. She wrote numerous novels, short stories, and poems that tackled various themes and subjects. Alcott's works often reflected her progressive views on women's rights, social justice, and the importance of individuality.

Throughout her life, Alcott remained dedicated to her family and their well-being. She continued to support them financially, even as her own success grew. Louisa May Alcott never married or had children of her own but found fulfillment in her relationships with her sisters and her role as an aunt to her niece and nephews.

Tragically, Louisa May Alcott's life was cut short. She passed away on March 6, 1888, at the age of 55, just two days after her father's death. However, her literary contributions and the impact of her work endure long after her passing.

Louisa May Alcott's legacy as an influential writer and feminist icon lives on. Her portrayal of strong, independent female characters in "Little Women" paved the way for future generations of women writers. The novel has been adapted into numerous stage plays, films, and television series, ensuring that Alcott's characters and stories continue to enchant audiences to this day.

A Look at Major Themes
from the works of Louisa May Alcott

An abolitionist and a feminist, Louisa May Alcott explored a wide range of themes in her works. Here are some of the major ones:

FAMILY AND SISTERHOOD: A central theme in many of Alcott's works is the importance of family and the bonds between siblings. The relationships and dynamics within families, particularly among sisters, are explored with depth and complexity. Alcott portrays the joys, challenges, and deep love that exist within these familial connections.

COMING-OF-AGE AND SELF-DISCOVERY: Alcott often delves into the journey of self-discovery and personal growth, particularly through the experiences of young women. Her characters navigate the transition from adolescence to adulthood, grappling with societal expectations, finding their own identity, and pursuing their passions and dreams.

GENDER ROLES AND WOMEN'S RIGHTS: Alcott was a progressive thinker and advocate for women's rights. Her works challenge traditional gender roles and highlight the limitations and injustices faced by women in society. Alcott's female characters strive for independence, intellectual fulfillment, and the right to pursue their own ambitions, often defying societal expectations.

SOCIAL JUSTICE AND PHILANTHROPY: Alcott's writing reflects her strong sense of social justice and compassion for the less fortunate.

She addresses issues such as poverty, inequality, and the plight of the marginalized. Alcott's characters engage in acts of philanthropy, working to improve the lives of those in need and championing the importance of empathy and kindness.

INDIVIDUALITY AND NONCONFORMITY: Alcott celebrates individuality and nonconformity in her works. Many of her characters resist societal pressures and embrace their unique qualities, challenging conventions and norms. Alcott encourages readers to embrace their own identities, follow their passions, and stay true to themselves.

LOVE, FRIENDSHIP, AND RELATIONSHIPS: Love and friendship are explored in various forms throughout Alcott's works. She delves into the complexities of romantic relationships, the enduring power of friendships, and the importance of emotional connections and support systems in navigating life's challenges.

EDUCATION AND INTELLECTUAL PURSUITS: Alcott valued education and intellectual pursuits, and these themes often find their way into her writing. She emphasizes the significance of learning, intellectual growth, and the pursuit of knowledge as a means of personal development and empowerment.

These themes, among others, contribute to the enduring appeal and relevance of Louisa May Alcott's works. Her exploration of these topics resonates with readers of different generations, making her writing timeless and impactful.

If you feel your value
lies in being merely
decorative, I fear
that someday you
might find yourself
believing that's all
that you really are.
Time erodes all such
beauty, but what it
cannot diminish
is the wonderful
workings of your
mind: Your humor,
your kindness, and
your moral courage.

(Little Women (1868))

Have regular hours
for work and play,
make each day both
useful and pleasant,
and prove that you
understand the worth
of time by employing
it well. Then youth
will be delightful,
old age will bring
few regrets, and life
become a beautiful
success, in spite of
poverty.

(Little Women (1868))

It takes so little to
make a child happy,
that it is a pity in a
world full of sunshine
and pleasant things,
that there should be
any wistful faces,
empty hands, or
lonely little hearts.

(Little Men (1871))

When women are the
advisers, the lords of
creation don't take the
advice till they have
persuaded themselves
that it is just what they
intended to do. Then
they act upon it, and,
if it succeeds, they give
the weaker vessel half
the credit of it. If it
fails, they generously
give her the whole.

(Little Women (1868))

It's amazing how
lovely common
things become,
if one only knows
how to look at them.

(Marjorie's Three Gifts (1899))

Honesty is the best
policy, in love
as in law.

(Little Women (1868))

When I had youth I had no
money; now I have the money
I have no time; and when I get
the time, if I ever do, I shall
have no health to enjoy life.
I suppose it's the discipline
I need; but it's rather hard to
love the things I do, and see
them go by because duty
chains me to my galley. If I
ever come into port with all
sails set, that will be my
reward perhaps.

(Louisa May Alcott: Her Life, Letters,
and Journals (ed. 1914))

I often think
flowers are the
angels' alphabet
whereby they write
on hills and fields
mysterious and
beautiful lessons for
us to feel and learn.

(Louisa May Alcott: Her Life,
Letters, and Journals (ed. 1914))

Simple, genuine
goodness is the best
capital to found the
business of this life
upon. It lasts when
fame and money fail,
and is the only
riches we can take
out of this world
with us.

(Little Men (1871))

A principle that can't
bear being laughed
at, frowned on, and
cold-shouldered,
isn't worthy of the
name.

(An Old-Fashioned Girl (1869))

Money is a needful and
precious thing, and when
well used, a noble thing,
but I never want you to
think it is the first or
only prize to strive for.
I'd rather see you poor
men's wives, if you were
happy, beloved, contented,
than queens on thrones,
without self-respect
and peace.

(Little Women (1868))

I've learned to check
the hasty words that
rise to my lips, and
when I feel that they
mean to break out
against my will, I just
go away for a minute,
and give myself a
little shake for being
so weak and wicked.

(Little Women (1868))

Love is a flower that
grows in any soil,
works its sweet
miracles undaunted
by autumn frost or
winter snow, blooming
fair and fragrant all
the year, and blessing
those who give and
those who receive.

(Little Men (1871))

Don't cry so bitterly,
but remember this
day, and resolve with
all your soul that
you will never know
another like it.

(Little Women (1868))

Beth ceased to fear
him from that moment,
and sat there talking
to him as cozily as if
she had known him all
her life, for love
casts out fear, and
gratitude can
conquer pride.

(Little Women (1868))

I like to help women
help themselves,
as that is, in my
opinion, the best way
to settle the woman
question. Whatever we
can do and do well we
have a right to, and I
don't think any one
will deny us.

(The Selected Letters of Louisa
May Alcott (ed. University of
Georgia Press, 1995))

Love is a great
beautifier.

(Little Women (1868))

People want to be
amused, not preached
at, you know. Morals
don't sell nowadays.

(Little Women (1868))

Now and then, in this
workaday world,
things do happen
in the delightful
storybook fashion,
and what a comfort
that is.

(Little Women (1868))

You may try your
experiment for a week
and see how you like
it. I think by Saturday
night you will find
that all play and no
work is as bad as all
work and no play.

(Little Women (1868))

Meg learned to love her
husband better for his
poverty, because it seem
to have made a man of him,
giving him the strength
and courage to fight his
own way, and taught him a
tender patience with
which to bear and comfort
the natural longings and
failures of those he loved.

(Little Women (1868))

I like good strong
words that mean
something.

(Little Women (1868))

Cheerfulness can
change misfortune
into love and
friends.

(Jack and Jill:
A Village Story (1880))

Don't try to make me
grow up before my time,
Meg. It's hard enough
to have you change all
of a sudden. Let me be a
little girl as long as I
can.

(Little Women (1868))

Simple, sincere
people seldom speak
much of their piety.
It shows itself in
acts rather than in
words, and has more
influence than
homilies or
protestations.

(Little Women (1868))

I don't know how long
it will last, but I'm
not afraid of storms,
for I'm learning how
to sail my ship.

(Little Women (1868))

I don't pretend
to be wise, but I am
observing, and I see a
great deal more than
you'd imagine. I'm
interested in other
people's experiences
and inconsistencies,
and, though I can't
explain, I remember
and use them for my
own benefit.

(Little Women (1868))

You have a good many
little gifts and virtues,
but there is no need of
parading them, for
conceit spoils the finest
genius. There is not much
danger that real talent
or goodness will be
overlooked long; even if
it is, the consciousness
of possessing and using
it well should satisfy
one, and the great charm
of all power is modesty.

(Little Women (1868))

If you dear little
girls would only learn
what real beauty is,
and not pinch and
starve and bleach
yourselves out so,
you'd save an immense
deal of time and money
and pain. A happy soul
in a healthy body makes
the best sort of beauty
for man or woman.

(Eight Cousins (1875))

Our actions are in
our own hands, but the
consequences of them
are not. Remember
that, my dear, and
think twice before
you do anything.

(Jack and Jill:
A Village Story (1880))

Education is not confined to books, and the finest characters often graduate from no college, but make experience their master, and life their book. [Some care] only for the mental culture, and [are] in danger of over-studying, under the delusion . . . that learning must be had at all costs, forgetting that health and real wisdom are better.

(Jo's Boys (1886))

A time will come when
you will find that in
gaining a brief joy
you have lost your
peace forever.

(A Long Fatal Love Chase
(published posthumously
in 1995))

If we are all alive
ten years hence,
let's meet, and see how
many of us have got
our wishes, or how
much nearer we are
then than now.

(Little Women (1868))

You are the gull, Jo,
strong and wild,
fond of the storm and
the wind, flying far
out to sea, and happy
all alone.

(Little Women (1868))

Have your fun, my
dear; but if you must
earn your bread, try
to make it sweet
with cheerfulness,
not bitter with the
daily regret that it
isn't cake.

(Jo's Boys (1886))

There are many Beths
in the world, shy and
quiet, sitting in
corners till needed,
and living for others
so cheerfully that no
one sees the sacrifices
till the little cricket
on the hearth stops
chirping, and the
sweet, sunshiny
presence vanishes,
leaving silence and
shadow behind.

(Little Women (1868))

I like adventures,
and I'm going to
find some.

(Little Women (1868))

Wild roses are
fairest, and nature
a better gardener
than art.

(A Long Fatal Love Chase
(published posthumously
in 1995))

She was one of those
happily created beings
who please without
effort, make friends
everywhere, and take
life so gracefully
and easily that less
fortunate souls are
tempted to believe
that such are born
under a lucky star.

(Little Women (1868))

It is the small
temptations which
undermine integrity
unless we watch and
pray and never think
them too trivial to be
resisted.

(Rose in Bloom (1875))

Fame is a pearl many dive for and only a few bring up. Even when they do, it is not perfect, and they sigh for more, and lose better things in struggling for them.

(Jo's Boys (1886))

Prosperity suits
some people, and
they blossom best in
a glow of sunshine;
others need the
shade, and are the
sweeter for a touch
of frost.

(Jo's Boys (1886))

Many of the bravest
never are known,
and get no praise.
[But] that does not
lessen their beauty...

(Louisa May Alcott: Work, Eight
Cousins, Rose in Bloom, Stories
& Other Writings (ed. Library of
America, 2014))

If I can do no more,
let my name stand
among those who are
willing to bear
ridicule and reproach
for the truth's sake,
and so earn some right
to rejoice when the
victory is won.

(letter to the American Woman
Suffrage Association in support
of women's voting rights, Oct.
1885)

Beth could not reason upon or explain the faith that gave her courage and patience to give up life, and cheerfully wait for death. Like a confiding child, she asked no questions, but left everything to God and nature, Father and Mother of us all, feeling sure that they, and they only, could teach and strengthen heart and spirit for this life and the life to come.

(Little Women (1868))

No, I never wish that.
I don't intend to die
till I've enjoyed my
life. Everyone has a
right to happiness and
sooner or later I will
have it. Youth, health
and freedom were meant
to be enjoyed and
I want to try every
pleasure before I am
too old to enjoy them.

(A Long Fatal Love Chase
(published posthumously
in 1995))

I put in my list
all the busy,
useful independent
spinsters I know,
for liberty is a
better husband than
love to many of us.

(Louisa May Alcott: Her Life,
Letters, and Journals (ed.
1914))

The patience and
the humility of the
face she loved so
well was a better
lesson to Jo than
the wisest lecture,
the sharpest
reproof.

(Little Women (1868))

I ask not
for any crown
But that which
all may win;
Nor try to
conquer any world
Except the one
within.

(The Complete Poetry by Louisa
May Alcott)

Life and love are
very precious when
both are in full
bloom.

(Little Women (1868))

In spite of the
laughing at them, the
world would never
get on without
reformers.

(Little Women (1868))

Keep good company,
read good books,
love good things and
cultivate soul and
body as faithfully
as you can.

(Rose in Bloom (1875))

The invigorating air did them both good, and much exercise worked wholesome changes in minds as well as bodies. They seemed to get clearer views of life and duty up there among the everlasting hills. The fresh winds blew away desponding doubts, delusive fancies, and moody mists. The warm spring sunshine brought out all sorts of aspiring ideas, tender hopes, and happy thoughts. The lake seemed to wash away the troubles of the past, and the grand old mountains to look benignly down upon them saying, "Little children, love one another."

(Little Women (1868))

We can't any of us do
all we would like,
but we can do our best
for every case that
comes to us, and that
helps amazingly.

(An Old-Fashioned Girl (1869))

One of the sweet
things about pain and
sorrow is that they
show us how well we
are loved, how much
kindness there is in
the world, and how
easily we can make
others happy in the
same way when they
need help and
sympathy.

(Jack and Jill:
A Village Story (1880))

The humblest tasks
get beautified if
loving hands do them.

(Little Women (1868))

Be comforted, dear
soul! There is always
light behind the
clouds.

(Little Women (1868))

He was poor, yet
always appeared to
be giving something
away; a stranger, yet
everyone was his
friend; no longer
young, but as happy-
hearted as a boy;
plain and peculiar,
yet his face looked
beautiful to many.

(Little Women (1868))

It is never too early to try and plant [good principles] in a child, and never too late to cultivate them in the most neglected person.

(Little Men (1871))

Gentlemen, be courteous to the old maids, no matter how poor and plain and prim, for the only chivalry worth having is that which is the readiest to pay deference to the old, protect the feeble, and serve womankind, regardless of rank, age, or color.

(Little Women (1868))

I've been so bothered
with my property,
that I'm tired of it,
and don't mean to save
up any more, but give
it away as I go along,
and then nobody will
envy me, or want to
steal it, and I shan't
be suspecting folks
and worrying about
my old cash.

(Little Men (1871))

"Christmas won't be
Christmas without any
presents," grumbled Jo,
lying on the rug. "It's so
dreadful to be poor!"
sighed Meg, looking down
at her old dress. "I don't
think it's fair for some
girls to have plenty of
pretty things, and other
girls nothing at all,"
added little Amy, with an
injured sniff. "We've got
Father and Mother, and
each other," said Beth
contentedly from her
corner.

(Little Women (1868))

The power of
finding beauty in
the humblest things
makes home happy
and life lovely.

(Jack and Jill:
A Village Story (1880))

I... resolved to take
Fate by the throat
and shake a living
out of her.

(Louisa May Alcott: Her Life,
Letters and Journals, Ednah
D. Cheney, ed. (1889))

...to the inspiration of
necessity, we owe half
the wise, beautiful,
and useful blessings
of the world.

(Little Women (1868))

Clothes possess
an influence more
powerful over many
than the worth of
character or the
magic of manners.

(Little Women (1868))

The child has talent, loves music, and needs help. I can't give her money, but I can teach her; so I do, and she is the most promising pupil I have. Help one another, is part of the religion of our sisterhood, Fan.

(An Old-Fashioned Girl (1869))

A holiday isn't a
holiday, without
plenty of freedom
and fun.

(Little Men (1871))

It takes three or four
women to get each man
into, through, and
out of the world.

(Jo's Boys (1886))

Love is the only
thing that we can
carry with us when
we go, and it makes
the end so easy.

(Little Women (1868))

I think she is
growing up, and so
begins to dream
dreams, and have
hopes and fears and
fidgets, without
knowing why or
being able to
explain them.

(Little Women (1868))

Men are always
ready to die for us,
but not to make our
lives worth having.
Cheap sentiment and
bad logic.

(Jo's Boys (1886))

Love scenes,
if genuine, are
indescribable;
for to those who have
enacted them the most
elaborate description
seems tame, and to
those who have not,
the simplest picture
seems overdone.

(An Old-Fashioned Girl (1869))

You are like a chestnut burr, prickly outside, but silky-soft within, and a sweet kernel, if one can only get at it. Love will make you show your heart some day, and then the rough burr will fall off.

(Little Women (1868))

Fathers and mothers
are too absorbed
in business and
housekeeping to study
their children, and
cherish that sweet and
natural confidence
which is a child's
surest safeguard,
and a parent's
subtlest power.

(Eight Cousins (1875))

The scar will remain,
but it is better for a
man to lose both arms
than his soul; and these
hard years, instead of
being lost, may be made
the most precious of
your lives, if they
teach you to rule
yourselves.

(Jo's Boys (1886))

Meg's high-heeled slippers were dreadfully tight, and hurt her, though she would not own it; and Jo's nineteen hair-pins all seemed stuck straight into her head, which was not exactly comfortable; but, dear me, let us be elegant or die.

(Little Women (1868))

Women have been
called queens for a
long time, but the
kingdom given them
isn't worth ruling.

(An Old-Fashioned Girl (1869))

Far away there in
the sunshine are my
highest aspirations.
I cannot reach them:
but I can look up,
and see their beauty;
believe in them, and
follow where they
lead.

(Work: A Story of Experience
(1873))

They were enjoying the
happy hour that seldom
comes but once in any
life, the magical
moment which bestows
youth on the old,
beauty on the plain,
wealth on the poor, and
gives human hearts a
foretaste of heaven.

(Little Women (1868))

I believe that it is as much a right and duty for women to do something with their lives as for men and we are not going to be satisfied with such frivolous parts as you give us.

(Rose in Bloom (1875))

I must know where you are,
but I will not molest nor
betray you till the time
arrives. Go where you like,
assume what disguise you
choose, do what you please,
except die or marry. I'll
stand off and watch the
play, but I must follow.
I like the chase, it is
exciting, novel and
absorbing. I have tried and
tried of other amusements,
this satisfies me and
I am in no haste to end it.

(A Long Fatal Love Chase (published
posthumously in 1995))

To be strong, and
beautiful, and go
round making music
all the time. Yes, she
could do that, and with
a very earnest prayer
Polly asked for the
strength of an upright
soul, the beauty of a
tender heart, the
power to make her life
a sweet and stirring
song, helpful while it
lasted, remembered
when it died.

(An Old-Fashioned Girl (1869))

There is very little
real liberty in the
world; even those who
seem freest are often
the most tightly bound.
Law, custom, public
opinion, fear or shame
make slaves of us all, as
you will find when you
try your experiment.

(A Long Fatal Love Chase
(published posthumously in 1995))

I was thinking what a
curious thing love
is; only a sentiment,
and yet it has power
to make fools of men
and slaves of women.

(A Long Fatal Love Chase
(published posthumously
in 1995))

A real gentleman is
as polite to a little
girl as to a woman.

(An Old-Fashioned Girl (1869))

Life is my college.
May I graduate well,
and earn some honors!

(Louisa May Alcott: Her Life,
Letters, and Journals)

And when they went
away, leaving comfort
behind, I think there
were not in all the city
four merrier people
than the hungry little
girls who gave away
their breakfasts and
contented themselves
with bread and milk
on Christmas morning.

(Little Women (1868))

The emerging woman ...
will be strong-minded,
strong-hearted,
strong-souled,
and strong bodied
...strength and beauty
must go together.

(An Old-Fashioned Girl (1869))

The first small
sacrifice of this sort
leads the way to others,
and a single hand's
turn given heartily to
the world's great work
helps one amazingly
with one's own small
tasks.

(An Old-Fashioned Girl (1869))

Power is a
dangerous thing.
Be careful that you
don't abuse it
or let it make a
tyrant of you.

(Jo's Boys (1886))

I tell you I cannot bear it! I shall do something desperate if this life is not changed soon. It gets worse and worse, and I often feel as if I'd gladly sell my soul to Satan for a year of freedom.

(A Long Fatal Love Chase (published posthumously in 1995))

Don't shut yourself up
in a band box because
you are a woman, but
understand what is
going on, and educate
yourself to take part
in the world's work,
for it all affects you
and yours.

(Little Women (1868))

We've got minds and
souls as well as hearts;
ambition and talents
as well as beauty and
accomplishments; and we
want to live and learn
as well as love and be
loved. I'm sick of being
told that is all a woman
is fit for! I won't have
anything to do with love
until I prove that I am
something beside a
housekeeper and a
baby-tender!

(Rose in Bloom (1875))

It takes very
little fire to
make a great deal
of smoke nowadays,
and notoriety is
not real glory.

(Jo's Boys (1886))

The small hopes and
plans and pleasures
of children should be
tenderly respected by
grown-up people,
and never rudely
thwarted or
ridiculed.

(Little Men (1871))

...marriage, they say,
halves one's rights
and doubles one's
duties.

(Little Women (1868))

Salt is like good-
humor, and nearly
every thing is better
for a pinch of it.

(Little Men (1871))

Well, I am happy, and
I won't fret, but it
does seem as if the
more one gets the
more one wants...

(Little Women (1868))

Many wise and true
sermons are preached
us everyday by
unconscious ministers
in street, school,
office, or home; even a
fair table may become a
pulpit, if it can offer
the good and helpful
words which are never
out of season.

(Little Women (1868))

Jo had learned that hearts, like flowers, cannot be rudely handled, but must open naturally.

(Good wives, a sequel to 'Little women' (1869))

Good books, like good friends, are few and chosen; the more select, the more enjoyable.

(Little Women (1868))

I'm tired of praise;
and love is very sweet,
when it is simple and
sincere like this.

(Jo's Boys (1886))

The duty we owe
ourselves is greater
than that we owe
others.

(Moods (1865))

Well, if I can't be
happy, I can be
useful, perhaps.

(Little Women (1868))

Girls are so queer
you never know what
they mean. They say
no when they mean
yes, and drive a man
out of his wits just
for the fun of it.

(Little Women (1868))

Don't laugh at the spinsters, dear girls, for often very tender, tragic romances are hidden away in the hearts that beat so quietly under the sober gowns, and many silent sacrifices of youth, health, ambition, love itself, make the faded faces beautiful in God's sight. Even the sad, sour sisters should be kindly dealt with, because they have missed the sweetest part of life, if for no other reason.

(Little Women (1868))

I don't like favors;
they oppress and make
me fell like a slave.
I'd rather do
everything for
myself, and be
perfectly
independent.

(Little Women (1868))

I think immortality is
the passing of a soul
through many lives or
experiences, and such
as are truly lived,
used and learned,
help on to the next,
each growing richer,
happier and higher,
carrying with it only
the real memories of
what has gone before.

Painful as it may be,
a significant
emotional event can
be the catalyst for
choosing a direction
that serves us - and
those around us -
more effectively.
Look for the
learning.

When Emerson's library was burning at Concord, I went to him as he stood with the firelight on his strong, sweet face, and endeavored to express my sympathy for the loss of his most valued possessions, but he answered cheerily, 'Never mind, Louisa, see what a beautiful blaze they make! We will enjoy that now.' The lesson was one never forgotten and in the varied lessons that have come to me I have learned to look for something beautiful and bright.

We all have our own life
to pursue, our own kind
of dream to be weaving,
and we all have the
power to make wishes
come true, as long as
we keep believing.